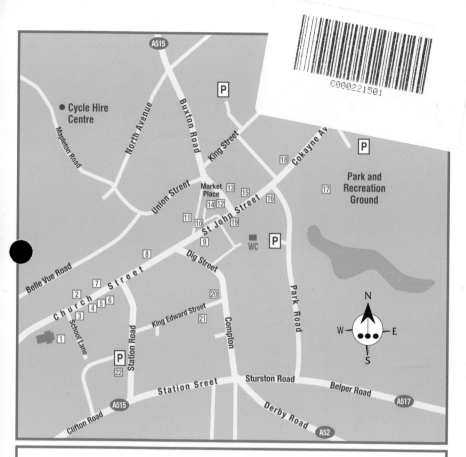

Ashbourne

1. St Oswald's Church
2. Former Queen Elizabeth's Grammar School
3. The Old Hall
4. The Mansion
5. Owfield's Almshouses
6. Pegg's Almshouses
7. The Grey House
8. Vine House
9. The Green Man & Black's Head Royal Hotel
10. Victoria Square
11. The Lamplight Restaurant
12. Market Place
13. Town Hall
14. Tourist Information
15. Former Green Dragon Inn
16. Madge House
17. Park & Recreation Ground
18. Ashbourne Library
19. Gingerbread Shop
20. Compton House
21. Bus Station
22. Swimming Pool & Leisure Centre

Top: Shrovetide Football in full swing   **Above:** Victoria Square

ASHBOURNE & AREA
Including Carsington Water

Introduction

Ashbourne has long been described as the Gateway to Dovedale, and the ancient market town is one of Derbyshire's finest with numerous attractions. Apart from its famous Royal Shrovetide Football Game and Ashbourne Gingerbread, it provides a feast of wonderful Georgian architecture, and St. Oswald's is one of the most impressive parish churches in the country.

Ashbourne was once an important staging post on the London to Manchester coach route, and inns such as the Green Man and Black's Head Royal Hotel in St John Street, linked by the unique gallows-style sign across the road, provide evidence of this prosperous past.

Ashbourne has been a natural focus for the villages of the southern White Peak at least since 1257, when its market charter was granted. The street market is still held every Thursday and Saturday on the cobbled, sloping market place at the top of the town. Every Shrove Tuesday and Ash Wednesday, the town is still taken over by the playing of Royal Shrovetide Football, a boisterous reminder of how association football began. Ashbourne is also the southern terminus of the famous Tissington walking and riding trail.

A stroll round Ashbourne

(the numbers in brackets refer to the town centre map on page 1)
The best way to appreciate Ashbourne's historic heart and architecture is to take a short stroll around its streets. Start with a visit to the Early English-style **parish church of St. Oswald** (1), one of the finest in the Peak and rated by architectural historian Sir Nikolaus Pevsner as "one of the grandest churches in Derbyshire."

The Victorian novelist George Eliot described St. Oswald's as "the finest mere parish church in the kingdom", and its slender 215ft/65m spire is the highest and most elegant in the Peak District. Eliot used Ashbourne as "Oakbourne" in her popular novel *Adam Bede*, part of which was set in "Stonyshire" – her fictional name for Derbyshire. For James Boswell, another regular visitor to the town with his friend, the famous

Above: Monument to Penelope Boothby, St Oswalds

Right: St Oswald's church

lexicographer Dr. Samuel Johnson of Lichfield, the church was "one of the largest and most luminous that I have seen in any town of the same size."

St. Oswald's is certainly one of the glories of Ashbourne. It stands on the site of a Norman minster church which was mentioned in the Domesday Book (where Ashbourne is named *Esseburn* or "ash tree stream"), but most of the present building dates from its rebuilding in the Early English style in the 13th century. There is a rare consecration brass of 1241 in the south transept. The tower and spire of the church were raised in the Perpendicular style in 1330–50, at the crossing of the nave and transepts.

The main part of the building still retains the classic Early English style, seen especially well in the south doorway with its ribbed moulding and dogtooth decoration. Unusually for a parish church, St. Oswald's has chapels to its transepts, which all adds to the spacious feeling it gives of being more like a small cathedral than Eliot's "mere parish church."

The alabaster monuments and tombs to the Cokayne, Boothby and Bradbourne families in the north transept chapel are justly famous, but perhaps the best-known monument in this wonderful church is that to Penelope Boothby of Ashbourne Hall, who died in 1791 at the tender age of five.

Thomas Banks's pure white Carrara marble figure of the child is so lifelike that she appears to be only sleeping, and Queen Charlotte is said to have broken down in tears when she saw the statue at a Royal Academy exhibition. The touching epitaph reads: "She was in form and intellect most exquisite. The unfortunate Parents ventured their all on this frail Bark. And the wreck was total." Allegedly, little Penelope's parents

Above: The Mansion

Left: Old Grammar School

separated at the child's grave and never spoke again. Nearby is Barrett's monument to Lady Boothby, who died in 1838.

Turning right out of St. Oswald's churchyard, across Church Street is the magnificent, sandstone-built **Old Grammar School** (2), which was founded in 1585 by Sir Thomas Cokayne on behalf of Elizabeth I. The present building was completed in 1603, and beneath the steeply-roofed gables, the long array of mullioned windows facing the street are fronted by pavement cobbles taken from the nearby River Dove. The school was located in the middle part of the building, and houses for the schoolmasters were at either end. A new grammar school was built in 1909 on Green Road, and the old school remained in use as a boarding house for boys until as recent as 1993.

Opposite the Grammar School are the classical Georgian fronts of **The Old House** (3) and **The Mansion** (4). The Old House has a Georgian façade on a much older building, which explains its irregular proportions with the front door on one side. The Mansion was built for Dr. John Taylor, another friend of Samuel Johnson (who was a regular visitor), in 1685. In 1764, an octagonal domed drawing room was added to the old house and the new façade of brick with a classical portico was built facing Church Street.

Next to The Mansion are two of the many almshouses which were established for the poor of the town during the 17th and 18th centuries. **Owfield's Almshouses** (5) were built as single-storey dwellings between 1610 and 1648, and the upper floor was added in 1848. At right angles to the street are the single-storey **Pegg's Almshouses** (6), built in 1669.

Top: Pegg's Almshouses
Above: The Grey House

Opposite Owfield's Almshouses is the dignified, stone-built edifice simply known as **The Grey House** (7). Built in 1750, its frontage has the same classical look of The Mansion just down the street, but is built in stone. The adjacent houses were once its stables.

On the same, northern side of Church Street stands **Vine House** (8) which was built in the early 18th century again on the foundations of a much older property. The vine still flourishes, and under the classical porticoed porch, you can still see the arched basement windows of the original Tudor building.

Further down St. John Street just beyond Dig Street you come to the rare sight of a "gallows" inn sign which crosses the road and advertises two former coaching inns – **the Green Man and the Black's Head Hotel** (9) – which were combined into one in 1825. Now known as **The Green Man and Black's Head Royal Hotel** the 'Royal' appendage commemorates the visit of Princess Victoria in the early 1830s. The carved head of a turbaned blackamoor, grinning on one side and looking gloomy on the other, occupies the centre of the archway.

The Green Man is the spiritual home of the town's annual Royal Shrovetide Football Game (see box opposite). The landlord allowed the game to be started (or "ball turned up") on his nearby field, Shaw Croft (now a car park) in 1863. It had previously been banned from taking place in the Market Place.

Ashbourne Royal Shrovetide Football

You can get a real idea of the origins of association football if you visit the normally peaceful market town on Shrove Tuesday and Ash Wednesday.

Town centre shop fronts are boarded up and traffic stopped as Ashbourne's boisterous Royal Shrovetide Football Game takes over the whole town. The two teams are known as the "Up'ards" and "Down'ards" with the Henmore Brook being the dividing line. The players are known as the 'hug' and they move in a huge, swaying, steaming crowd to score at their own 'goals' which are set three miles apart. These were originally at Sturston Mill and the former Clifton Mill. As both mills are now demolished two new goals have been provided. Both are in the river and the scorer has to be in the water to goal the ball.

The 'turner-up' is called upon to start the proceedings at 2pm on the Shaw Croft. The decorated leather, cork-filled ball is then tossed into the crowd. The designs on the ball show the particular interests of the 'turner-up' along with the Imperial Crown and Union Flag. The ball can then be grabbed by the opposing teams and kicked, carried and hugged through the streets, with steam rising off the bodies of the players in the general hectic scrum. At some stage numerous players seem to end up in the Henmore Brook.

If a ball is scored before 5pm a second ball is turned up. If the ball is scored after 5pm the game finishes, if it is not scored then play continues until 10pm. The player who goals the ball keeps it, but if the ball is not goaled then the 'turner-up' keeps it.

Balls on display in Ashbourne Ex-Servicemen's Club

Top: The Green Man and Black's Head Royal Hotel, St John Street

Above left: Victoria Square at Christmas

Above: Ashbourne Town Hall

Left: Market day

Opposite the Green Man on the left, the sloping **Victoria Square** (10) leads up to the 16th century former **Tiger Inn** (11), now the Lamplight Restaurant, housed in one of Ashbourne's oldest buildings. Its gable projects onto the street adjacent to Tiger Yard. This is a very old thoroughfare which leads to Dove House Green a name which possibly recalls a medieval village green.

Victoria Square leads up to Ashbourne's cobbled, triangular **Market Place** (12). Here weekly markets have been held since the 13th century and still take place every Thursday and Saturday. Ashbourne's market was first recorded in 1257, and it was created a borough by Edward I in 1281. In 1745, Prince Charles Edward Stuart – "Bonnie Prince Charlie" – declared his father, King James III, in the Market Place. This was on his fateful march on London which was finally to end in ignominious retreat at Derby.

Overlooking the Market Place is the balconied Victorian Gothic **Town Hall** (13), which was originally built as the Market Hall in 1861. Also in the Market Place is the **Tourist Information Centre** (14) located in a former shop dating from the 18th century.

Returning back down to St. John Street, a left turn will take you to the former **Green Dragon Inn** (15), a timber-framed building which claims to be Ashbourne's oldest. Almost opposite is **St. John's Hall**, which was formerly the Magistrates' Court. At the end of St. John Street at the junction with Park Road stands **Madge House** (16) where the daughters of Erasmus Darwin, grandfather of the great evolutionist Charles Darwin, once ran a school.

Beyond here on the right is Ashbourne's **Park and Recreation Grounds** (17), which were once the park of Ashbourne Hall in Cokayne Ave. The Hall is now partly demolished and serves as **Ashbourne Library** (18). The park features a large fish pond, tennis courts, picnic benches and a children's play area.

Returning down St. John Street you will see the **Ashbourne Gingerbread Shop** (19) on your left (see box p.10). Continue on to turn left into Dig (originally Ditch) Street, crossing the Henmore Brook by Compton Bridge. Here you will see one of Ashbourne's largest and finest buildings, the gracious **Compton House** (20). Now serving as a bank, Compton House was the town house of the locally-important Beresford family, and was built around 1770.

Ashbourne Gingerbread

Usually rolled out and made into the fairytale shapes of Gingerbread Men, Ashbourne Gingerbread has a long and fascinating history. The original recipe is said to have been brought to the town by the personal chef of a captured French general. He was held in the town in 1805 during the Napoleonic wars.

The timber-framed Gingerbread Shop in St John Street, now owned by Birds the Confectioners, probably dates from the 15th century. Ashbourne Gingerbread is available today from Birds and Spencer's Bakery in the Market Place.

There are numerous varieties of gingerbread, cakes and puddings, but this recipe comes from John Dunstan's book of Old Derbyshire Desserts.

Ingredients
8 oz self-raising flour; 2 tsp ground ginger; 1 tbsp golden syrup; 4 oz butter; pinch of salt; 4 oz brown sugar

Method
1. Preheat oven to 350F/gas 4.
2. Sieve flour, salt and ginger together.
3. Cream the syrup, butter and sugar together then stir in the dry ingredients.
4. Knead the mixture on a floured surface into a smooth dough.
5. Roll out and cut into shape required.
6. Place on a greased baking tin and bake until brown for about 15-20 minutes depending on the thickness.

King Edward Street, adjacent to Compton House, gives access to the town's **Bus Station** (21), and the **Swimming Pool and Leisure Centre** (22) on the site of the town's former railway station. This was the southern terminus of the former Ashbourne to Buxton railway line, which opened in August 1899. All that remains now is the imposing stone-built former goods warehouse in Clifton Road. The former railway line now serves as the Tissington Trail walking and riding leisure route (see box p.12).

Carsington Water

There are few lakes in the porous limestone countryside of the White Peak, so the construction of Carsington Water Reservoir in 1992 created a great opportunity for recreational water-lovers. Today, the 741 acre/300ha reservoir has a thriving sailing club and facilities for windsurfing, canoeing and fishing, and there is a cycle hire centre which enables you to pedal around its shores.

There's an adventure playground for children, and for nature lovers, the reservoir provides an important wetland habitat for many water-loving species of animals, birds and insects, including occasional visiting ospreys. A visit to the Wildlife Centre, near the Visitor Centre, is also worth doing. You can watch the bird life in warmth and comfort using the binoculars that are available. Children particularly love it here.

Carsington Water was opened by the Queen in 1992 and has become one of the most popular visitor attractions in this part of the Peak. It is the ninth largest reservoir in England and at its highest level can hold 7,800 million gallons of water – enough to fill all the Derwent, Howden and Ladybower reservoirs in the Upper Derwent Valley – or to keep one person supplied with water for over half a million years!

Carsington stores water pumped from the River Derwent at times of high rainfall, and is owned and operated by Severn Trent Water.

Carsington Water Visitor Centre is open daily, except Christmas Day (☎ 01629 540696; website: www.stwater.co.uk)

Tissington Trail

If you are feeling energetic, you can hire a bike from the Cycle Hire Centre in Ashbourne and go for a cycle along the 11½ mile/18km Tissington Trail. The converted former railway line winds up over the limestone plateau, with spectacular, traffic-free views on all sides.

The trail was created as a walking and riding route by the Peak District National Park Authority in 1968, after the former Ashbourne-Buxton line, which opened in August 1899, closed. The line was designed to double track standards, but was only built as a single track, and in later years was little more than a branch line carrying passengers and local freight between the two towns. The line finally fell under the Beeching axe in September, 1967.

Unfortunately, the National Park Authority demolished the five stations along the route, leaving only the Hartington Signal Box, which served for many years as an information and ranger briefing point, complete with its array of signal levers.

There are numerous picnic sites and parking places along the Trail between Ashbourne and Parsley Hay, creating plenty of opportunities to stop and admire the stunning White Peak scenery.

Cycle hire

The Peak District National Park Cycle Hire Centre in Mapleton Lane, Ashbourne (☎ 01335 343156; website: www.peakdistrict.org/cycle), provides access to the Tissington Trail, with the pretty well-dressing village of Tissington a three-mile cycle ride away. There is another cycle hire centre where the Tissington Trail joins the High Peak Trail at Parsley Hay, (☎ 07961 052 590), north-east of Hartington.

The Ashbourne centre has a range of books, maps and cycling-related products for sale and friendly and knowledgeable staff are on hand to offer help and advice. An emergency cycle repair service is also offered although this may not always be available. Car parking (pay and display – free to blue badge holders) is available on site along with refreshments, picnic tables and toilets (including disabled facilities).

A short ride through a tunnel (complete with railway sound effects) brings you out in Ashbourne town centre.

PLACES OF INTEREST AROUND ASHBOURNE

Dovedale

Dovedale is perhaps the most famous of the White Peak dales, but perhaps best avoided on Bank Holiday weekends when the large car park soon fills up, and a constant stream of walkers file through its narrow confines. But the startling rock formations, rising clear out of the ash woodlands, such as the Tissington Spires, Ilam Rock and Pickering Tor, are worth the effort at other times on the easy, three-mile path through the dale. This was where Izaak Walton and Charles Cotton, of nearby Beresford Hall, conceived and wrote the fisherman's bible, *The Compleat Angler*, in 1653.

Top: Thorpe Cloud, Dovedale
Above: Stepping stones, Dovedale

Thor's Cave, Manifold Valley

The Manifold Valley

Parallel to Dovedale in Staffordshire is the quieter Manifold Valley, easily reached from Ilam or Grindon. Its rock features such as Beeston Tor and the awesome gaping void of Thor's Cave – the archetypal caveman's dwelling – are as impressive as anything in Dovedale. Further up the dale on the Manifold Track, the bulk of Ecton Hill contains the Peak's only copper mine, the profits from which enabled the 6th Duke of Devonshire to construct the famous Crescent at Buxton.

Ilam Park

Ilam Park

Ilam Park (National Trust) is set beside the River Manifold, and enjoys outstanding views towards the hills of Dovedale and walks into the Manifold Valley. Here the river, like other limestone rivers in the Peak, disappears underground during the summer months. There is a well-appointed information centre and tea-room.

Wells blessing, Tissington

Tissington

The first of the Peak District villages to celebrate well dressings is the pretty limestone village of Tissington. Here the custom was first recorded in 1758 and five wells are dressed at Ascensiontide. The village is dominated by two buildings, the stately, 18th century mansion of Tissington Hall open to the public, and the Parish Church of St. Mary with its squat tower, on the hill opposite.

Tissington Hall has been the home of the FitzHerbert family for 400 years. It was built by Francis FitzHerbert in 1609 to replace a moated manor house to the north of the church and is now open to the public. There is an award-winning tea room in the Old Coach House nearby.

Just across the road from Tissington Hall is the Parish Church of St. Mary with its squat tower. The church dates back to Norman times and has an interesting Norman font and many monuments to the FitzHerbert family.

Hartington

Hartington is centred on the square with its restored mere (pond), and is a convenient centre for exploring the Dove Valley. Tudor Hartington Hall, just outside the village, is allegedly the place where Bonnie Prince Charles stayed on his ill-fated march on London in 1645, and is now a beautifully-restored youth hostel. You can actually stay in the bedroom where allegedly, the ill-fated prince slept.

Formerly the home of Long Clawson Dairy Ltd off the village square, Hartington was one of a few places in England qualified to produce the tasty, blue-veined Stilton cheese. It is still sold in the village's specialist cheese shop in Stonewell Lane but no longer produced in the village.

Above: Hartington village
Left: Hartington Hall
Below: Morris men at Hartington Wakes Week

FURTHER INFORMATION

Events in the Ashbourne Area

Shrovetide Football: Shrove Tuesday and Ash Wednesday, Shaw Croft Car Park, 2pm

Tissington Well Dressing: Ascension Day until the following Wednesday

Ashbourne Arts Festival: End June to early July (www.ashbournefestival.org email info@ashbournefestival.org)

Ashbourne Highland Gathering: July

Ashbourne Shire Horse Society Agricultural Show: Mid-August

Other useful information

Ashbourne Leisure Centre
Clifton Road, Ashbourne
☎ 01335 343712; email: ashbourneleisurecentre@derbyshiredales.gov.uk

Tourist Information Centre (due to close in 2013)
13 Market Place, Ashbourne
☎ 01335 343666; website: www.visitpeakdistrict.com

Market days: Thursdays and Saturdays in the Market Place

Car Parks: Pay & Display at Shaw Croft, the Leisure Centre and off King Street. There is a free car park off Cokayne Avenue at the Adult Education Centre

Toilets: Main one on Shaw Croft Car Park. Also in the Bus Station, Recreation Ground and Union Street but these may close in the future

All information is correct at the time of printing

Acknowledgements

Photography

© **Mark Titterton** Front cover; back cover top-left; p.2bottom; p.4all; p.8mid-left; p.13all; p.14all; p.15all
© **Edward Rokita** Back cover top-mid & top-right; p.5left; p.6bottom; p.8top mid-right & bottom; p.11
© **Lindsey Porter** p.2top; p.5right; p.6top; p.7
© **Ruth Downing (Rural Pictures)** Back cover bottom
© **Sarah Wyatt** p.10

Special thanks to
Visit Peak District, Peak District Tourist Information – www.visitpeakdistrict.com

Published by **Ashbourne Editions**
10 Queen Elizabeth Court, Belle Vue Road, Ashbourne DE6 1NE
Tel: (01335) 344882 Mobile: 07890 854634

1st edition: ISBN: 978-1-873-775-42-4

© **Roly Smith 2012**

Print Gomer Press, Llandysul, Wales **Design** www.ceibagraphics.co.uk